If you were a
PLUS
SIGN

by Trisha Speed Shaskan
illustrated by Francesca Carabelli

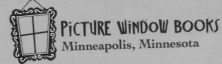

PiCTURE WiNDOW BOOKS
Minneapolis, Minnesota

plus sign (+) a symbol used to show addition

Editor: Christianne Jones
Designers: Nathan Gassman and Hilary Wacholz
Page Production: Melissa Kes
The illustrations in this book were created with acrylics.

Picture Window Books
151 Good Counsel Drive
P.O. Box 669
Mankato, MN 56002-0669
877-845-8392
www.picturewindowbooks.com

Printed in China

102009
005561

Library of Congress Cataloging-in-Publication Data
Shaskan, Trisha Speed, 1973-
If you were a plus sign / by Trisha Speed Shaskan ;
illustrated by Francesca Carabelli.
p. cm. — (Math fun)
Includes index.
ISBN 978-1-4048-4784-2 (library binding)
ISBN 978-1-4048-4785-9 (paperback)
ISBN 978-1-4048-6172-5 (saddle-stitched)
1. Mathematical notation—Juvenile literature.
2. Addition—Juvenile literature. I. Carabelli, Francesca,
ill. II. Title.
QA41.S482 2009
513.2'11—dc22
                                    2008006458

Special thanks to our
advisers for their expertise:

Stuart Farm, M.Ed., Mathematics Lecturer
University of North Dakota

Terry Flaherty, Ph.D., Professor of English
Minnesota State University, Mankato

If you were
a plus sign . . .

3

... you would help add things together.

Ida plus Ike equals true love.
They make a family of two. $1 + 1 = 2$

Ida and Ike have a cub called Ina.
They make a family of three. **2+1=3**

Ida, Ike, and Ina love pets. They have two seals.
They make a family of five.

$$\begin{array}{r} 3 \\ +2 \\ \hline 5 \end{array}$$

5

If you were a plus sign, you would be a symbol used to show addition. You would be part of an addition problem.

Selma juggles five red balls plus two green balls. That's a total of seven balls.

$$\begin{array}{r} 5 \\ +\,2 \\ \hline 7 \end{array}$$

Trigg jumps through four blue hoops plus four purple hoops. That's a total of eight hoops.

4 + 4 = 8

If you were a plus sign, you would be used like the word "and."

Doodle gives Pluck three daisies and six roses. Three and six equals nine.

$$
\begin{array}{r}
3 \\
+\ 6 \\
\hline
9
\end{array}
$$

Pluck gives Doodle one valentine and eight chocolates. One and eight equals nine.

$$1 + 8 = 9$$

If you were a plus sign, you would help make a sum. The sum is the total of two or more numbers.

$$5 + 5 = 10$$

Five bulldogs met five tigers to play basketball at the park. They made a sum of ten players.

Six bulldogs plus six tigers showed up to cheer them on. They made a sum of twelve cheerleaders.

$$\begin{array}{r} 6 \\ + 6 \\ \hline 12 \end{array}$$

If you were a plus sign, you could work left to right or top to bottom.

$$4 + 3 = 7$$

Spotty cooks four blueberry pancakes for herself and three plain pancakes for Dotty.

Spotty stacks the three plain pancakes and the four blueberry pancakes on a plate.

$$\begin{array}{r} 3 \\ + 4 \\ \hline 7 \end{array}$$

If you were a plus sign, you could add in any order and still get the same sum.

A frightened frog leaps across four lily pads and then bounces onto two more lily pads. He jumps on six lily pads altogether.

$$4+2=6$$

A frightened frog leaps across two lily pads and then bounces onto four more lily pads. He jumps on six lily pads altogether.

$$\begin{array}{r} 2 \\ + 4 \\ \hline 6 \end{array}$$

If you were a plus sign, you could add any amount of numbers. You could add two, three, four, or more. You would get the same sum no matter how the numbers were arranged.

Five elephants plus four hippos plus three rhinos equals twelve show animals.

5 + 4 + 3 = 12

$$\begin{array}{r} 5 \\ 3 \\ +\ 4 \\ \hline 12 \end{array}$$

Five elephants plus three rhinos plus four hippos equals twelve show animals.

If you were a plus sign, you could add small numbers or big numbers.

Gert wears eight red bracelets on her right arm and eight pink bracelets on her left arm. Gert is wearing sixteen bracelets.

$$8+8=16$$

Gert has thirteen bows on her tail and fourteen bows in her mane. She's wearing twenty-seven bows.

$$13+14=27$$

Gert has 100 polka dots on her skirt, and Stretch has 100 triangles on his vest and tie. Together, they have two hundred shapes on their clothes.

$$100+100=200$$

If you were a plus sign, you could help solve story problems.

Cherry juggles five red balls. She adds three green balls and two orange balls. How many balls does Cherry juggle in all?

5+3+2=10

Cherry juggles ten balls in all.

21

You would always help add things together ...

... if you were a plus sign.

ADDITION REVIEW

It's time to use that plus sign and review! Throughout the book you have added a lot of different items. Now grab a piece of paper and a pencil. Solve the addition problems below.

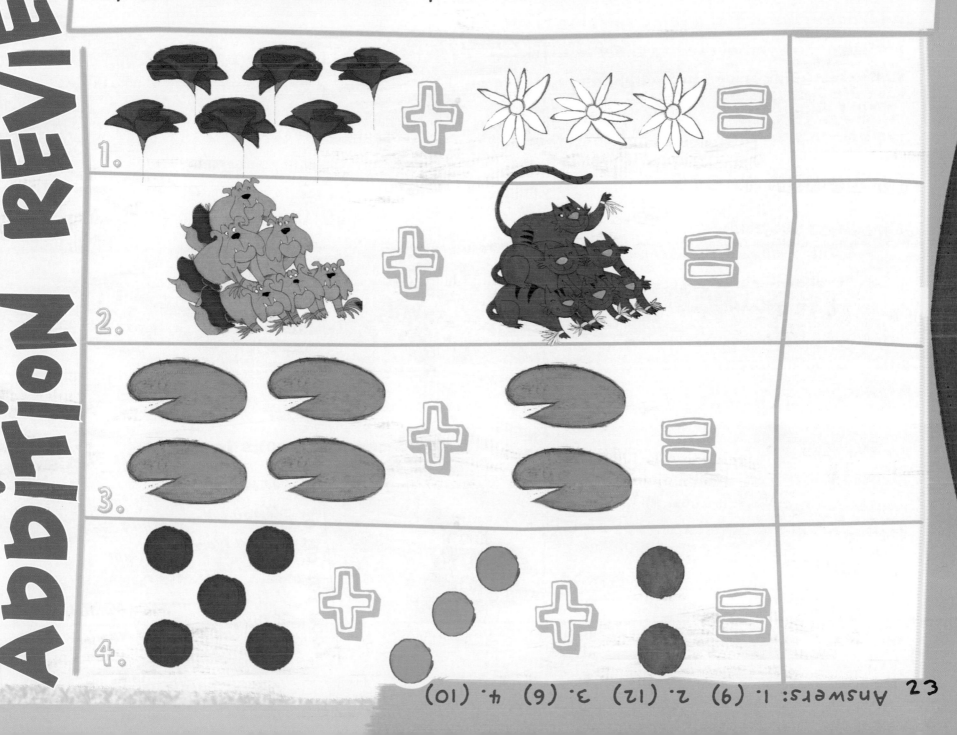

Answers: 1. (9) 2. (12) 3. (6) 4. (10)

Glossary

add—to find the sum of two or more numbers

addition—the act of adding numbers together

plus sign—a symbol used to show addition

sum—the number you get when you add two or more numbers together

symbol—a sign that stands for something else

To Learn More

More Books to Read

Bauer, David. *Adding Arctic Animals*. Bloomington, Minn.: Yellow Umbrella Books, 2004.

Cleary, Brian P. *The Mission of Addition*. Minneapolis: Millbrook Press, 2005.

Gisler, David. *Addition Annie*. New York: Children's Press, 2002.

On the Web

FactHound offers a safe, fun way to find Web sites related to topics in this book. All of the sites on FactHound have been researched by our staff.

1. Visit *www.facthound.com*
2. Type in this special code: 1404847847
3. Click on the FETCH IT button.

Your trusty FactHound will fetch the best sites for you!

Index

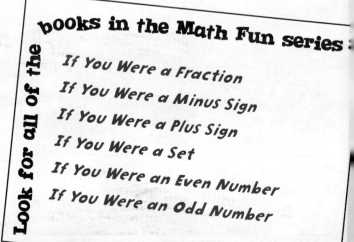

Look for all of the books in the Math Fun series:

If You Were a Fraction
If You Were a Minus Sign
If You Were a Plus Sign
If You Were a Set
If You Were an Even Number
If You Were an Odd Number